SACAJAWEA

BRAD PHILLIPS

THE WAYSIDE BOOKSHOP

Published by:
Apricot Press
Box 1611
American Fork, Utah
84003

books@apricotpress.com
www.apricotpress.com

ISBN 1-885027-29-X

Printed in the United States of America

Cover: Lewis and Clark at Three Forks
E.S. Paxson
Oil on Canvas, 1912
Courtesy of the Montana Historical Society
Don Beatty photographer 10/1999

Introduction

First things first. This book is called Sacajawea. It could have just as easily have been titled Sacagawea, Sakakawea, Porivo, or The Indian Formerly Known As Sacajawea. We don't know for sure what she was called, so I picked the name that most Americans, including myself, were taught in grade school.

Sacajawea was an oddity among the members of the Lewis and Clark expedition. She was the only woman, the only full-blooded Indian, along with her husband she was one of only two non-English speakers, and of course, she was the only mother. Lewis and Clark were heading into territory no white man had ever seen. Sacajawea was going home. And there is one more critical difference. With the exception of Clark's slave, she was the one person who did not choose to be there. The men of the expedition were on the adventure of their lives and they knew it. Lewis and Clark had picked them from among hundreds of eager volunteers to be the first white men to cross the continent. They knew they were fortunate to be participants. They also anticipated "great rewards" when they returned. They were exactly where they wanted to be.

Sacajawea was not free to make these types of choices. Through her entire life, it is unlikely that any man ever asked her where she wanted to go or what she wanted to do. She was an Indian and a woman—the lowest possible status in 19th Century America, other than slave. In the journals, she is rarely even mentioned by name. She is "the squaw," "the Snake woman," "our Indian woman," or "the squaw wife of the interpreter." It would never have occurred to anyone, even her husband, to ask her preference. She probably would have been bewildered had someone inquired.

Her low social standing in no way diminishes her contributions to the expedition—if anything, it amplifies them. If we knew her thoughts and more of her story, she would likely be recognized as an even greater heroine than she is today. Sadly, we don't have the autobiography of Sacajawea. We have to learn about her through the eyes of men who surely did not understand her—linguistically or culturally—and only slowly learned to appreciate her value.

- Brad Phillips

Contents

Illustrations

A well-armed Minnetaree raiding party like this one would have brought terror to Sacajawea's Shoshone tribe. The painting is "The Return of the War Party" by Frederic Remington.

Photo from the Library of Congress, Prints and Photographs Division, LC-USZ62-98462.

Chapter 1

Three Forks

Three Forks, Montana
Summer 1799

Panic erupted in the Shoshone teepees at the sight of a Minnetaree raiding party. Every Shoshone, even the youngest, understood the danger. The Minnetarees were after three items: horses, slaves, and scalps. They would show no mercy. Women immediately began herding their children away from the open village, up the west fork of the river, and into the relative safety of the trees.

Once hidden in the forest, the Minnetaree raiders would have a difficult time finding the well-camouflaged Shoshone. Horses would have improved their survival chances immeasurably but Shoshone women and children did not ride. Horses were reserved for the men. The

Six years later, Meriwether Lewis would name this fork the Jefferson River after the President who sent him to explore the West. At the time of this Minnetaree raid, Jefferson was living comfortably at his home at Monticello. He had recently retired from politics and claimed to have no interest in the Presidency of the United States.

1

warriors mounted their horses and rode out to face the Minnetarees as best they could. This type of battle required a unique brand of bravery. There was no question which tribe would be victorious. The Shoshone men had been repeatedly beaten by the Minnetaree. The warriors knew they could only delay not defeat the marauders. They also knew that no captured Shoshone man would be allowed to live. Unlike women and children, the Minnetarees never took warriors as slaves. The only issue was whether the men could impede the Minnetarees long enough time to allow their families to traverse the perilous three miles to the forest unharmed.

The life of the Lemhi Shoshone had not always been like this. Previous generations had hunted the buffalo on the plains without fear. Now, that was all changed. Three centuries earlier, the Spanish had brought horses to North America. Soon, the Shoshones had become some of the most skilled horsemen among all the Indians and had acquired huge herds of fine horses. However, the horse was a mixed blessing. It allowed the Shoshones to expand their territory and to hunt more successfully, but horses brought new and powerful enemies. The Minnetarees, also known as the Hidatsa, came from 500 miles away—present North Dakota—to steal the Shoshones' horses and capture their women and children for slaves. The Blackfeet encroached on their territory from the north. To make matters worse, these tribes had firearms. The British and French had moved south from Canada and developed a lively trade supplying the Blackfeet, Sioux, Mandans, and Minnetarees with guns and whisky in exchange for pelts. Distant forces the Shoshone could not even know about, let alone change, were conspiring to bring about their doom.

> When Meriwether Lewis saw the Shoshone horses, he compared them favorably with his own herd—a high compliment from a Virginia planter.

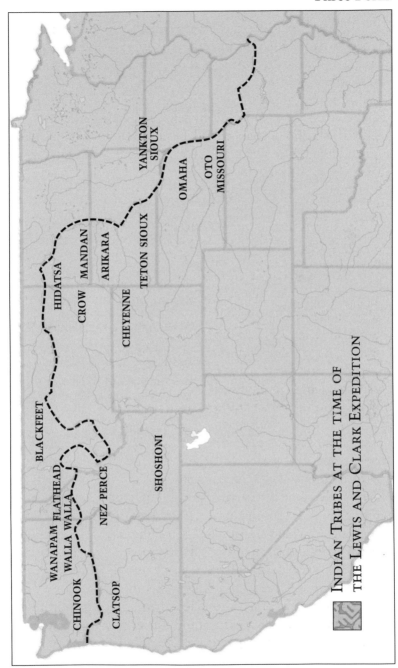

INDIAN TRIBES AT THE TIME OF
THE LEWIS AND CLARK EXPEDITION

The arrival of the Europeans, along with their horses and weapons, had forced the Shoshone into a nomadic existence. During the winter, they camped high on the eastern side of the Rocky Mountains. There was little game. Roots, berries, and fish were the staples of their diet. Here they lived on the edge of starvation but safely hidden from their enemies. When the buffalo came in the spring, the Shoshones risked a hazardous journey onto the plains to obtain meat and hides. During the summer, they would have enough to eat but only at the peril of their lives.

The Lemhi Shoshone referred to themselves as the "Agui Dika," or salmon-eaters.

At the Three Forks of the Missouri, this small band of Indians had lost the yearly gamble that each Shoshone had to make between safety and starvation. The warriors fought desperately to defend their families. They were better horsemen than the Minnetarees and their horses were stronger and quicker, but their bows and arrows were no match for guns. The rifles were more lethal and had a greater range than any of the Shoshone weapons. Four men were killed--a tremendous loss for the tribe. Still, the warriors bought enough time for some of the women and children to make it into the forest. The Minnetarees plunged into the woods after them. A few of the women and children fled deeper into the woods and were able to escape. Some stayed still and managed to go unnoticed. The less fortunate were massacred or taken prisoner.

After seeing her mother killed, one 12-year-old girl made a frantic dash across the river. Perhaps while the raiders were busy searching the woods she could slip away unnoticed. She was halfway to the opposite bank when she heard the splashing of horse hooves behind her. A powerful hand grabbed her deerskin tunic and lifted her churning legs out of the water. The warrior slung her across his horse and raced

back to join his companions. Sacajawea was now a
Minnetaree slave.

Swiss artist Karl Bodmer painted this portrait of a Minnetaree warrior
between 1839-1841. He is wearing a ceremonial costume for the Dog
Dance. Photo from the Library of Congress, Prints and Photographs
Division, LC-USZC4-4804.

The Minnetaree did not take Shoshone men as slaves. Slavery as practiced by the Minnetarees was very different from the type of slavery practiced by men like Lewis and Clark. The inefficient agricultural system of the South was predicated on inexhaustible and cheap supplies of land and labor. Land could be taken from the Indians. Labor could be taken from the slaves. Young, strong men were the most valuable of all slaves because they could do the most work. The slaveholder viewed his slaves as an asset, little different from a horse or a plow.

The Minnetarees did not have the inclination or the means to subjugate an entire class of people to do their farming. They obtained the labor of the Shoshone slaves by assimilation. Young girls and boys were incorporated into the villages through adoption or marriage. This increased the size and strength of the tribe. The difficult life of the Shoshone instilled them with a strong work ethic that made them useful to the Minnetaree. A Shoshone warrior could never be brought into the tribe in this way and, as a result, would be a constant threat to escape or attack his captors. The Shoshone slaves soon learned that the Minnetaree lived safely and always had enough to eat. The Shoshone nickname for the Minnetaree was "Big Bellies," because their stomachs were always full. This was in marked contrast to the Shoshones' usual lifestyle. In general, the Minnetaree treated slaves with more respect than other slave-holding Indian tribes or Southern plantation owners.

Sacajawea was kidnapped at a site similar to this near the Three Forks of the Missouri River. Photo by the author.

Chapter 2
Lewis and Clark Make a Deal

Fort Mandan
Winter 1804-1805

Lewis and Clark had been extremely lucky. None of the European powers wanted an American expedition exploring disputed territory in North America. Jefferson called Lewis' mission a purely scientific venture but all the foreign powers knew the President was lying. Jefferson's true motivation was finding a water route across the continent. He wanted to control commerce and make the United States rich. Naturally, no European power wanted the expedition to start, let alone succeed. Then, just before the expedition was to venture onto foreign soil, Napoleon decided to sell the French portion of the continent to the United States. Now Lewis and Clark would be exploring primarily in their own country. That should have pacified the Europeans. It didn't. The Spanish denied Lewis permission to proceed from St. Louis until the Louisiana Purchase was final. In the meantime, they assembled a military company to stop the Americans. Luckily, the combined Spanish and Comanche force arrived at the Platte River a few weeks behind Lewis and Clark.

Another stroke of good luck came when the expedition

William Clark by Charles Willson
Peale, from life, 1807-1808
Courtesy of Independence
National Historical Park

Meriwether Lewis by Charles
Willson Peale, from life, 1807
Courtesy of Independence
National Historical Park

first met the Teton Sioux. The Sioux decided that the
presents offered by Lewis and Clark were insufficient. Three
Sioux warriors grabbed the towline of the boat that Clark was
piloting, and informed the captain that the Indians would be
keeping the boat and all the trade goods it contained as the
toll for continuing upriver unmolested. Clark drew his sword
and explained that the Americans were not to be treated as
"squaws." He explained that the expedition "must and would
go on." The Sioux notched their arrows and pointed them at
the men in the boat. Back on the expeditions' large keelboat,
Lewis loaded the cannons and aimed them at the Sioux. One
Sioux arrow would have likely meant the death of Clark and
the end of the expedition. At this moment, luck intervened
again. One of the Sioux chiefs, Black Buffalo, called his men
off. He asked that the Americans stay a few more days and
join the tribe for the scalp dance. Relations were tense for the
next few days but the expedition managed to pass through
Sioux territory without a casualty on either side.

As opposed to the nomadic teepee-dwelling Indians, the Mandans lived in permanent earth lodges, pictured here on the bluff. In the foreground are women riding in "bullboats." These craft were simply constructed by stretching a buffalo hide over willow branches. Sacajawea lived in a village like this from the time she was kidnapped until she left with Lewis and Clark. Photo from the Library of Congress, Prints and Photographs Division, LC-USZ-62-28804.

At winter quarters, along the Knife River in present North Dakota, the expedition got lucky again. They met a French-Canadian trapper named Toussaint Charbonneau. Charbonneau made a strong first impression. He was an experienced woodsman. He had lived among the Indians and spoke Minnetaree. Most importantly, his two wives—Sacajawea and Otter Woman—were both Shoshone. When the expedition reached the headwaters of the Missouri, they would need horses to cross the continental divide. The Shoshones were their best and probably their only hope for obtaining them. Having a Shoshone interpreter might prove invaluable. Lewis and Clark made arrangements to have Charbonneau join the expedition as a paid interpreter. His pregnant, teenage wife would come along as well.

Was Sacajawea Charbonneau's wife or his slave? The short answer is that in Indian society, of which the trappers were a part, there was barely a fine line between wife and slave. Sacajawea had become a Minnetaree slave as a young girl. Sometime between 1799 and 1804, she was acquired by Toussaint Charbonneau. We don't know for sure whether he won her in a contest or traded goods for her. Sacajawea was a commodity because she was a slave, but also because she was a woman. In most Indian tribes, any woman could be bought, sold, rented, or traded. There was no notion of romantic love or chivalry.

As a general rule, the Indian men hunted and fought. The women prepared the food and hides, planted and tended crops, and did many other physically demanding jobs that were considered squaws' work. Sacajawea's life with Charbonneau was certainly not pleasant but it was not much different than the life of other Shoshone or Sioux women. In some ways, Charbonneau's relative wealth as a white man would have made her life easier.

Once Sacajawea bore Charbonneau a son her status changed. If only for practical reasons, she couldn't be traded to another man. The birth of a child made their relationship more akin to a marriage although there was certainly no ceremony performed and Sacajawea was never consulted.

During the brutally cold winter of 1804-1805, Charbonneau and his wives lived in relative comfort at Fort Mandan with Lewis and Clark. In February, Sacajawea delivered a son, Jean Baptiste Charbonneau. Lewis was present at the birth, which was long and painful. One of Charbonneau's fellow trappers, Jessaume, suggested that they administer a potion made from rattlesnake tail. Lewis happened to have one. He crushed it and mixed it with water

11

for Sacajawea. She delivered ten minutes later. Ever the skeptic, Lewis wrote in his journal that, "This remedy may be worthy of future experiments, but I must confess that I want faith as to it's efficacy."

The next month, Charbonneau met with the captains to revise the terms of his contract. He must have realized his value, or more accurately Sacajawea's value, to the expedition. His terms were steep. Charbonneau did not want to share any of the everyday responsibilities of the enlisted men. He would not post guard duty. He wanted to have access to as many supplies as he decided to carry. Finally, if Charbonneau became dissatisfied with any man in the expedition, he would be free to return at any time. The captains agreed to none of these conditions. They immediately kicked him out of Fort Mandan. Charbonneau had seriously misjudged the character of the men with whom he was negotiating. Regardless of his importance, Lewis and Clark were not going to let some mountain man stipulate the provisions of his employment. Charbonneau took four days to swallow his pride and agree to all of the captains' terms. He never tried to assert his position again.

What games of chance did the Indians play? Indians enjoyed betting on many of the same competitions that we still have today: wrestling, shooting, and racing on foot or on horseback. When Lewis and Clark shot through what the native tribes considered to be the non-navigable rapids of the Clearwater River, the Indians bet on where the canoes would crash and sink. The favorite contest of the Plains Indians was the hand game. The rules were simple. Two teams sat on opposite sides of a log. Every man held a stick as a counter. One team had a set of carved bones that could be easily concealed in a man's hand. The leader of one team would then pass out the bones as his team sang songs and beat the log with sticks. The men would pass, or pretend to pass, the bones between each other. The leader of the opposing

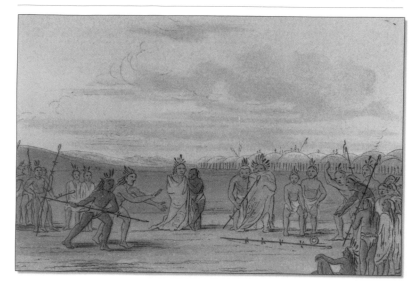

During the winter that Lewis and Clark spent at Fort Mandan, they observed the Mandans playing a game called "tchung-kee." According to Sergeant Ordway's journal, they used a pole to roll a hoop. Ordway couldn't determine exactly how the game was scored. Neither could George Catlin, who drew this sketch in the 1830's. Catlin did note that "these people become excessively fascinated with it; often gambling away everything they possess, and even sometimes, when everything else is gone, have been known to stake their liberty upon the issue of these games, offering themselves as slaves to their opponents in case they get beaten." Used by permission, Utah State Historical Society, all rights reserved.

team then had to guess which men were holding bones. If he guessed correctly, his team received the bones. When he was wrong, he lost one of his team's counting sticks. To win the game, one team had to collect all the counting sticks from their opponent. These games could take hours, or even days. The participants could bet hides, horses, weapons, or women; just about any possession could be wagered. There is a story told, most likely a tall tale, about a Sioux and a Crow warrior that played an especially high stakes session of the hand game. The Sioux was unlucky. He lost his knife, his bow, and his clothes. He was finally left naked without a single possession. Like many a modern gambler though, he knew his luck was about to change. He asked the Crow if he could bet his own scalp against his former possessions. The bet was accepted. The unfortunate Sioux warrior then watched with horror as the Crow pointed at his left hand—the one holding the bone. He sat silently as the Crow traced a line around his head with a scalping knife and, with a sudden jerk, removed his hair. Bleeding and delirious but still alive and still certain his luck would change, the Sioux demanded a rematch the next day. The Crow agreed. Sure enough, the Sioux warrior's luck improved. He won back all his possessions and even took the Crows' scalp. The Crow then bet the only possession he had left—his life. He lost again. This day, the Crow sat silently and stoically as the Sioux plunged a knife into his chest. For the rest of his life the Sioux warrior wore two scalps— his own and the Crows'—dangling from each ear.

On April 7, 1805, Captains Lewis and Clark, Clark's slave York, Charbonneau, Sacajewea, their two-month old son, and 27 soldiers set out to explore unknown territory. They would later call themselves the Corps of Discovery—an appropriate name. Until this date, they had been covering ground that had been previously described by a handful of white men. From here on they had no maps and only vague descriptions from Indians about what lay ahead. The only member of the expedition who had seen this territory before was the teen-aged wife of their French interpreter.

Is "Sacajawea" a historically correct name? No, it's not. Sacajawea was born a Shoshone, and we know for sure that "Sacajawea" is not a Shoshone name. When the Minnetarees kidnapped her they may have given her a Minnetaree name. "Sacajawea" is most likely a corruption of some type of Minnetaree word that may mean "Bird Woman." That is the most that can be said with certainty.

There were no pictures or drawings made of Sacajawea during her lifetime. No one who knew her bothered to write about her physical appearance. When Lewis and Clark met Sacajawea, she may have looked something like this young Cheyenne girl, photographed by Edward Curtis in 1905. Photo from the Library of Congress, Prints and Photographs Division, LC-USZ62-83569.

Lewis and Clark attempted a phonetic spelling of her name that appears to be pronounced "Sacagawea" though that is hardly definitive evidence. Modern linguists have debated whether the correct rendering of her name in Minnetaree should be "Sacagawea" or "Sakakawea." That is really beside the point. She would probably have responded to neither of those names and may well have resented the label given to her by her captors. Her correct name is an issue unlikely to ever be solved. Merle Wells, insightfully observes that, "Inflicting a more authentic Hidatsa (Minnetaree) name upon her scarcely can be defended as an appropriate activity for twentieth-century Lewis and Clark historians."

Chapter 3

Danger on the Trail

The Upper Missouri River
April-June 1805

The Corps of Discovery set out from Fort Mandan on April 7, 1805 in two large canoes, called pirogues. One of the captains usually stayed with the men and the boats while the other explored along the shore, searching for new plants and animals. Clark was the better waterman and Lewis the better botanist, so the typical arrangement was Lewis on land and Clark on the river. On those days that they reversed the pattern and Clark stayed on shore, he usually chose to explore with Charbonneau and Sacajawea. At first, this was probably because they were most familiar with the land. Charbonneau was an experienced trapper and woodsman. Sacajawea was an Indian. Clark wisely chose to learn what he could from them. Before long, a friendship developed between the Charbonneau family and

> In the journals, the pirogues were distinguished by their color. The larger pirogue was referred to as the "white pirogue." It was the more stable craft and carried the journals, medicines, and most valuable supplies. The smaller boat was called the "red pirogue."

17

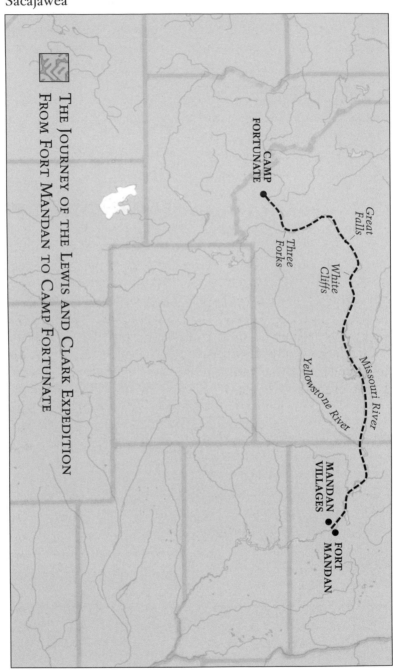

The Journey of the Lewis and Clark Expedition
From Fort Mandan to Camp Fortunate

Clark that lasted many years beyond the return of the expedition. Clark even found a nickname for Sacajawea: "Janey."

Unfortunately, this pattern was broken just a week into the trip and a disaster nearly ended the expedition. Sacajawea was in the white pirogue with Lewis. Charbonneau was at the helm. Suddenly, a gust of wind struck the sail and turned the ship sideways. Charbonneau panicked. Instead of turning the boat into the wind, he turned it broadside. Another gust of wind would have immediately capsized the boat. All of the expedition's papers, medicine, instruments, and most valuable trading goods would have been lost. The waves were high and it was almost 200 yards to shore. Lewis speculated that Sacajawea, her baby, and the three non-swimmers in the boat-including Charbonneau-would have surely drowned. True to form, good fortune intervened. At that moment the wind died for an instant. Lewis ordered Drouillard to push Charbonneau out of the way and take the helm. The other men quickly pulled the sails down. Before the wind hit again the pirogue was righted. After yet another close call, Lewis had to be wondering how much longer his luck would hold.

> Lewis preferred to explore with his dog or the half-Shawnee George Drouillard.

How did Sacajawea care for her baby while on the trail? Sacajawea must have been an incredible mother. She carried and cared for a baby on an adventure that taxed the survival skills of experienced mountain men. She probably carried Pomp on her back in a cradleboard. He would have been wrapped tightly inside with only his head able to move. When Sacajawea was cooking or doing other chores, she could lean the cradleboard against a tree and keep an eye on the baby. Instead of diapers, she set cattail cotton inside the cradleboard where Pomp

19

was sitting. The cotton was easily replaced as it became dirty and was very soft and absorbent.

Three Shoshone women surround an infant in a cradleboard. Sacajawea used a cradleboard like this one to carry Little Pomp from North Dakota to the Pacific Ocean and back. Used by permission, Utah State Historical Society, all rights reserved.

A month later he found out. On May 14th, Charbonneau was again at the helm. Why the captains allowed this after his earlier poor performance is anybody's guess. On this occasion, Lewis and Clark were both on shore—a rare occurrence. They watched in horror as the events of the previous month repeated themselves. A violent squall turned the boat. As before, Charbonneau took precisely the wrong action and turned the boat broadside. The wind whipped the sail out of the hands of the crew. The pirogue tilted and water rushed in, soaking the cargo. Lewis and Clark fired their guns to attract the men's attention. They screamed instructions from shore. "Cut the ropes!" "Haul in the sail!" But the men were too far away to hear. Lewis threw off his gun and shot pouch, and started stripping off his jacket in preparation to swim to their assistance. Either reason or Clark stopped him before he risked certain death to make the attempt. It was nearly a minute before the men were able to take in the sail. By that time water had filled the boat to within an inch of the top of the gunwales. Medicine, gunpowder, journals, and more were floating down the Missouri River. Worse, Charbonneau had still not righted the boat. He had abandoned the rudder and instead of trying to save the pirogue he was "praying to his god for mercy." The half-Omaha Pierre Cruzatte ordered Charbonneau to do his duty. It was useless. Charbonneau had already given himself up for dead. Cruzatte pointed his rifle at Charbonneau's head and repeated the order. There is nothing quite like staring into the barrel of a loaded gun to clear one's head. After Cruzatte's sincere threat, Charbonneau collected himself and finally grabbed the

> Charbonneau was an experienced trapper so it is hard to imagine that he was unfamiliar with canoes. The pirogues, however, were much bigger and required different skills to control. His tendency to panic probably stemmed from his inability to swim--a major difficulty for a trapper.

rudder. Meanwhile, Sacajawea gathered the small items that were floating away from the boat and would have undoubtedly been lost otherwise. By the time the pirogue made it to shore it was barely above water and every item on board was soaked. The expedition paused for two days to dry out and re-pack all the provisions. The loss of medical supplies was the most serious. They also lost some gunpowder and food. Two days later, Lewis singled out Sacajawea for praise: ". . . the Indian woman to whom I ascribe equal fortitude and resolution, with any person onboard at the time of the accedent, caught and preserved most of the light articles that were washed overboard." Perhaps in gratitude, Lewis named a tributary of the Musselshell River for Sacajawea six days later.

When the expedition left Fort Mandan, the captains considered Sacajawea's primary value to be as a Shoshone interpreter. As the incident with the pirogue proved, she had much more to offer. During the first few days away from Fort Mandan, there was little game. The Mandans and Minnetarees had scared the animals away with frequent hunting. Sacajawea used a digging stick to find Jerusalem artichokes to feed the men. Weeks later, when the hunters were bringing in hundreds of pounds of meat every day, the roots and berries that Sacajawea gathered helped provide a balanced diet.

On one day, June 2, 1805, the expedition's hunters brought in six elk, two buffalo, two mule deer, and a bear— over a ton of meat. The bear did not go quietly. The wounded grizzly chased Drouillard and Charbonneau. Charbonneau was able to hide in some bushes until Drouillard finally managed to kill the bear with a well-placed shot to the head. Numerous misadventures like these had instilled Lewis with a healthy respect for the grizzly. He confided in his journal that he would rather fight two Indians than one bear.

Captain Clark and his men shooting Bears.

Sergeant Patrick Gass was the first member of the Corps of Discovery to publish an account of the expedition. This drawing of "Captain Clark and His Men Shooting Bears" is from that 1810 volume. More than once, Charbonneau was nearly killed by a bear. Photo from the Library of Congress, Prints and Photographs Division, LC-USZ-62-19233.

Chapter 4
The Great Falls

From the Marias River to Beaverhead Rock
June-August 1805

On June 3rd, the expedition faced "an interesting question," as Lewis phrased it. Actually, it was more than an interesting question, for the success of the journey depended on the correct answer. The Missouri split into two branches. The south fork was clear, rapid, and full of stones. The north fork was muddy and deep. Lewis noted that the waters of the north fork "run in the same boiling and roling manner which has uniformly characterized the Missouri throughout it's whole course so far." Despite that similarity, Lewis and Clark both believed the south fork to be the true Missouri. Every member of the expedition disagreed. The decision was too momentous to risk to opinion. Taking the wrong fork meant missing the continental divide and, more than likely, reaching the Rocky Mountains too late to attempt a passage. The captains split the party and explored about twenty miles up each fork. Neither party could determine the true Missouri. Finally, the captains trusted their instincts and took the south fork. The men all believed they were following the wrong course but "cheerfully" followed the captains; at least that's what Lewis thought. In private moments the men may not have been so cheerful.

Did Sacajawea guide the expedition? The popular conception of Sacajawea has been as the Indian guide on whom Lewis and Clark relied to lead the way. Paintings show her arm outstretched, pointing to the next destination. Sacajawea was a valuable member of the Corps of Discovery but she was not their guide. Their guide was the Missouri River, and later, the Salmon, Snake, and Columbia Rivers. She was able to offer help occasionally and identify some landmarks but the captains did not rely on her.

On the occasions when the expedition truly needed a guide, she knew little more than the white men. Sacajawea was only a young girl when she was taken and the Shoshone did not travel widely on the plains because of their vulnerability to enemies. At the Marias River, she presumably disagreed with the captains, along with the rest of the party. At the Great Falls, a Nez Perce guide could have told them to ride west on horseback to reach the continental divide in five days. Instead they followed the river and wasted almost two months. Later, it was the Nez Perce and an old Shoshone man who helped the expedition across the Rockies.

Lewis rushed ahead with a small party to search for the Great Falls of the Missouri. If they had chosen the correct river, the expedition would soon be in Shoshone country, and Sacajawea could fulfill her crucial role as interpreter. There was only one problem. Sacajawea was deathly ill. She was feverish and, at times, delirious. Clark was worried. Lewis was the more knowledgeable doctor, but here was a patient that had to be cured and Lewis was already miles ahead of him and his return date was uncertain. Clark tried bleeding her. The treatment seemed to help at first but the next day her condition was even worse. Clark moved her to the covered

This statue shows Sacajawea in a typical, but inaccurate, pose pointing Lewis and Clark in the right direction. Used by permission, Utah State Historical Society, all rights reserved.

part of the pirogue so she could be out of the sun. For the next three days, Sacajawea's health continued to deteriorate. She hardly slept. Charbonneau wanted to take her and return to the Minnetarees. Whether this was a compassionate gesture toward his suffering wife or a selfish wish to go home is difficult to say.

The next day, Lewis returned with fantastic news. The Great Falls was just a few days ahead. The captains had chosen the correct fork. But Lewis' celebration was short-lived. Clark told him about Sacajawea and immediately relinquished his duties as physician. Now it was Lewis' turn to be worried. Sacajawea's pulse was irregular and faint. Her fingers and arms twitched spasmodically. She was clearly near death. Her death would be a catastrophic loss. They would be left with a motherless four-month-old baby to care for and without a Shoshone interpreter. Lewis declared her "our only hope for a friendly negociation with the Snake Indians on whom we depend for horses."

Bleeding her had clearly not been effective. Lewis would have to get creative. He decided to treat her with the water from a nearby sulfur spring. Lewis also gave

The Shoshone Indians were often referred to as Snake Indians because of the squiggly hand signal used to signify their name.

her two doses of bark and opium. Two years before, just before he went west, Lewis had spent nearly a month in Philadelphia learning medicine from one of leading physicians of the day, Dr. Benjamin Rush. Lewis had learned enough to know that he didn't know very much. His first goal was always to obey the Hippocratic oath and do no harm. If he managed to heal someone, so much the better. Some of his treatments, like bloodletting, were either ineffective or harmful. In this case, Clark's bleeding had depleted Sacajawea's blood of iron. The sulfur water probably helped replenish her.

The same day Lewis started this treatment, Clark added a tantalizing twist to the story in his journal. Apparently, Sacajawea had become delirious, probably from the fever and had refused to take her medicine. Obviously, this threatened her recovery, but once Charbonneau prevailed on her, she was easily convinced to take the treatment. The journals are unclear about how many days this situation had persisted. Clark was furious with Charbonneau, apparently for not taking a more active role in his wife's treatment. He wrote: ". . . if She dies it will be the fault of her husband as I am now convinced."

Fortunately for everyone, she didn't die. By the next day Sacajawea had improved considerably. The fever subsided and her pain was much better. The following day also brought improvement. Three days after Lewis' return Sacajawea was able to gather and eat some raw breadroot and dried fish. This diet was contrary to doctor's orders and Charbonneau drew Lewis' wrath for knowingly allowing her actions. Sacajawea's fever returned almost immediately and Lewis feared all his work had been undone. He gave her some saltpeter. By the following day she was improving. Within a week, Lewis pronounced her fully recovered.

The proximity of a sulfur spring at exactly the time they needed the water to save Sacajawea from death has to rate as yet another of the many fortunate circumstances that enabled the Corps of Discovery to make it to the Pacific.

While Sacajawea was recovering, the rest of the expedition was preparing for the difficult portage around the Great Falls. They cached the white pirogue and as many supplies as they could spare. The red pirogue was fitted with wheels, cut from a large cottonwood tree, and axles from the mast of the white pirogue. They loaded the inside with supplies and pushed and pulled across the rough ground. One windy day, the men raised the sail and let the breeze push the boat over dry land.

On June 29th, they ran into a tremendous hailstorm. Some of the stones measured seven inches in diameter and bounced 10-12 feet into the air as they landed. The men were out in the open without hats, some without even shirts. All they could do was run for cover. The hailstones knocked the men down as they fled. Some were nearly killed; most of the others were bruised and bloody.

Clark was away from the main party when the storm hit, walking along the river with Charbonneau and Sacajawea. As soon as the wind picked up, he decided to get away from the river so they would not be blown in. Clark led the small group to shelter under some overhanging rocks in a nearby ravine. Sacajawea pulled Pomp out of his cradleboard and held him close as they waited for the storm to pass. Suddenly, the heavens opened and water started roaring down the ravine. They rushed to get away from the oncoming torrent of water, rocks, and mud. Charbonneau was in the lead and managed to scramble up a hill. Sacajawea, carrying Pomp, and Clark, pushing Sacajawea, trailed behind. The water was rising fast around Clark's legs. He pushed Sacajawea up to Charbonneau. Then he pulled himself out of the floodwaters, with the water now roiling around his waist. Almost immediately the water rose to ten feet and by the time they reached the top of the hill, it was at fifteen. Pomp's cradleboard and nearly all of his clothing were washed away. Clark lost most of the equipment he had been carrying, including his compass. Miraculously, they found it the next day.

The expedition was delayed three weeks during the Great Falls portage. Time was now becoming critical. They had to find the Shoshone, trade for horses, and get across the mountains before snow made them impassable. As days passed and no Indians were encountered, the men became concerned. Sacajawea provided some hope, as she was occasionally able to identify the country. On July 22nd, she told the party that they were on the river where her people lived and that the Three Forks of the Missouri were near. This news raised the spirits of the men. Three days later, they reached the landmark and named the three rivers for President Jefferson and two Cabinet members, Secretary of Treasury Gallatin and Secretary of State Madison.

The Corps of Discovery was now camped exactly on the spot where Sacajawea had been kidnapped five years earlier. In reflecting upon this coincidence in the journals, Lewis makes an enigmatic comment about Sacajawea that deserves further discussion: "I cannot discover that she shews any immotion of sorrow in recollecting this event, or of joy in being again restored to her native country; if she has enough to eat and a few trinkets to wear I beleive she would be perfectly content anywhere." This entry is unusual in that Lewis rarely, if ever, commented on the mindset of any member of the expedition. Sacajawea's attitude likely drew special attention because she was an Indian.

Was Lewis' observation correct? Probably not. He was not well qualified to read the emotions of a person from a different sex, culture, and language. Did Lewis expect Sacajawea to break down in tears at the sight of the Three Forks? As any human being would, she doubtlessly felt sadness at the separation from her family and longing to be reunited. As an Indian woman, however, she would have had a much more fatalistic attitude toward the tragic events in her life like the kidnapping.

Two weeks later, on August 8th, Sacajawea identified another landmark. It was a large rock rising from the plain, called the "Beaver's Head" by the Shoshone because of the shape. She said that her people would be on this river or the nearby river to the west. That was all the encouragement Lewis needed. The next day he took a small party and rushed ahead to find the Shoshone. It was a tremendous risk. The Shoshones would be wary of any strangers. They would assume that strangers were there to take scalps and slaves as the Blackfeet and Minnetaree always did. The logical course of action for the Shoshones would be to slaughter the small group of white men or flee to the mountains and hide. Lewis' only hope was to somehow convince them that he was a friend. Luckily, he had had the foresight to bring a Shoshone interpreter a thousand miles to help. Unluckily, or foolishly, he didn't take Sacajawea with him to meet her people. He trusted his own ability to communicate with signals and Drouillard's ability to use sign language. The only precaution Lewis took was to ask Sacajawea to tell him the Shoshone word for "white man." There was no such word. She told him, "tababone," which means "stranger." Armed with a couple rifles, a few gifts, and a single, mistranslated word, Lewis rode out to meet the Indians on whom the fate of the expedition would depend.

Chapter 5

Return to the Shoshone

From Camp Fortunate to Shoshone Winter Camp
August 1805

While Lewis searched for Sacajawea's people, Clark led the bulk of the expedition slowly up the shallow and winding Jefferson River (today's Beaverhead River). Four to five miles a day was good progress. By August 14th, they reached Rattlesnake Cliffs, a site Lewis had already passed four days earlier. Here Clark saw Charbonneau strike Sacajawea. This was probably not an uncommon occurrence in a trapper-Indian marriage but it outraged Clark. He immediately came to her defense and gave Charbonneau a severe reprimand. There is no record of Charbonneau ever repeating such an offense. The next morning Clark and Sacajawea discovered why Lewis had named the campsite Rattlesnake Cliffs. They were both nearly bitten.

Eight days after Lewis' small search party had left, the expedition viewed an ominous sight. Several Indians came riding toward camp. Upon closer inspection, one of the "Indians" was Drouillard. He was dressed in Indian attire and an Indian was holding his rifle. Had the other men been killed? Were they hostages? Drouillard quickly answered

This photograph of Heebe-tse-tse, a Shoshone Indian, was taken around 1899. The fate of the Lewis and Clark expedition hung in large measure on friendly relations with this tribe. The captains brought Sacajawea along as an interpreter. Photo from the Library of Congress, Prints and Photographs Division, LC-USZ-62-102137.

their questions. Lewis, Shields, and McNeal were with the Shoshone. Lewis had promised the tribe that Clark would be waiting with gifts and trade goods at the forks of the Jefferson River just a few miles ahead. The Indians trusted Lewis, for the present, but any delay in Clark's appearance might cause them to rush back into hiding. This was welcome news. Clark hurried ahead to meet the Shoshones, along with Sacajawea.

How did Lewis convince the Shoshones to come to Camp Fortunate? Lewis saw his first Shoshone just two days after splitting with Clark. The single, young warrior stayed a cautious distance away from the white men. Lewis stripped off his shirt to show his white skin, laid out a blanket and trades goods, and began shouting, "Tababone!" Meanwhile Shields and Drouillard approached the Indian from each side. Lewis knew this would spook him and tried to call his men back. Shields couldn't hear. The Shoshone, fearing a trap, turned his horse and disappeared. Lewis despaired of ever seeing another. Two days later, however, they found a small group of Shoshone women. The women, sure of imminent death, hung their heads in preparation for the blow. Instead, Lewis showered them with presents. The women lead Lewis to a nearby party of sixty warriors who successively embraced each of the four white men. By the time the ceremony was over, Lewis was so smeared with grease and paint that he pronounced himself "heartily tired of the national hug."

When they reached the Indian camp, Sacajawea was finally reunited with her people. She looked for familiar faces and quickly found a girlhood friend. They ran towards each other and joyfully embraced. Sacajawea and her friend had both been kidnapped at the same time by the Minnetarees. Together they had endured the terror and deprivations of that ordeal and provided comfort for each other. Somehow, her friend had managed to escape and made her way back home, never thinking she would see Sacajawea again. Lewis described this reunion as "peculiarly touching." The young woman he had described as nearly emotionless just a few weeks before was now almost overcome.

The captains immediately convened a council with the Shoshone chief Cameahwait. Now that Sacajawea was present they could communicate more freely and negotiate for horses. Translating was still no simple feat. Sacajawea knew Shoshone and Minnetaree but not English or French. Charbonneau spoke French and Minnetaree, but poor English. Labiche spoke French and English. Thus, Sacajawea translated from Shoshone to Minnetaree for Charbonneau, who then translated into French for Labiche. Labiche translated into English for Lewis and Clark. The cycle was reversed for Cameahwait.

Soon after this meeting began, Sacajawea jumped from her place and ran towards the chief. She hugged him, threw her blanket around his shoulders, and started crying. This reaction was more than just happiness to see her chief again. During the translation process, Sacajawea had recognized Chief Cameahwait as her own brother. This was a coincidence beyond belief. As Stephen Ambrose writes in *Undaunted Courage*, "no novelist would dare invent such a scene." Naturally, Cameahwait was thrilled to see his sister and grateful to Lewis and Clark for her safe return. Successful trading negotiations were all but inevitable. To celebrate their good luck, they named their campsite Camp Fortunate.

One reunion was not quite as fortunate. Many years earlier, Sacajawea's father had promised her to a Shoshone man in exchange for some horses, as was the custom. This warrior now stepped forward to claim his bride. This is another instance where the journals are maddeningly sparse on details. This must have been an emotional moment. Was Sacajawea excited to have an Indian husband and live with her own people? Was Charbonneau willing to fight for his wife?

The site of Camp Fortunate, where Sacajawea was reunited with her people, is now at the bottom of the Clark Canyon Reservoir. In 1805, the barely navigable Beaverhead River split into two impassable streams at this point. The men left the water and headed across the Rocky Mountains by foot and, if the Shoshones were willing to sell, by horse. Photo by author.

We don't know. Lewis only mentions the episode in passing and states that since Sacajawea had already born children, her Shoshone fiancé lost interest in her. He probably didn't want to be responsible for feeding another man's child.

What was it like to be a Shoshone? At the time Lewis and Clark encountered the Shoshones, they were a culture in serious distress. They lived a semi-nomadic existence, alternately moving between salmon country and buffalo country. From May to August, they lived off salmon caught in the high tributaries of the Columbia River. When the salmon runs ended, they risked a dangerous journey to the plains of southwest Montana where they killed and jerked enough buffalo to last them through the winter. Even to survive on meager rations they required about 15 tons of buffalo meat. Their many horses were necessary to hunt and transport the meat to the winter camp. The men of the expedition noticed very few elderly people. After just five years, all but two members of Sacajawea's family were dead. Few people could survive this difficult life for long.

The unexpected appearance of Lewis and Clark and the miraculous return of his sister put Cameahwait in a difficult position. The white men desperately needed horses to get across the mountains. They also needed guides and logistical help getting across Lemhi pass. In exchange for this assistance, the explorers had only meager trade goods. The one commodity that the Shoshone needed most—guns—was something the expedition would not, or could not, spare. Yet Captain Lewis promised that if the Shoshones would help the expedition, white traders would return and set up a supply post near their home. This promise filled Cameahwait and all the Shoshones with hope. With guns, they could defend themselves against the Blackfeet and Minnetarees. They could hunt the buffalo at will and not have to hide in the mountains through the freezing winters. All these competing demands and responsibilities played upon his mind. He could spare the horses though it would be a sacrifice. He did not know if he could spare the time. His people were starving and his first obligation was to them.

Lewis knew firsthand how close to starvation the Shoshones actually were. Just the day before the reunion at Camp Fortunate, Drouillard had killed a deer. When word spread, the Shoshones whipped their horses mercilessly to reach the kill site. Lewis was carrying a Shoshone warrior on his horse who was lashing the horse harder than Lewis could tolerate. When Lewis reined in the horse, the starving Indian jumped off and sprinted nearly a mile to the dead animal. By the time Lewis arrived the deer was nearly devoured. The Indians were eating the deer like "famished dogs." The kidneys, liver, intestines, and every other part of the deer were eaten immediately and raw. Lewis was knowingly asking Cameahwait to make his people go hungry another several weeks when buffalo country was just a few days ride away.

Cameahwait finally agreed to go back to his village (near present Tendoy, Idaho) and return with additional horses. The captains sent Sacajawea with her brother in the hope that she could hurry the Indians along. Lewis stayed behind at Camp Fortunate with most of the men to cache everything possible and prepare for the trip across the mountains. He had to wait only four days for the Shoshones to return. At this point, Cameahwait must have felt he had done everything possible for the white men, but Lewis needed more. Lewis had only been able to trade for about a dozen horses. He would need many more to carry his men and supplies over the Rockies. Lewis extracted a promise from Cameahwait to help the expedition make it as far as the Shoshone winter village. On August 24th, the Corps of Discovery left Camp Fortunate, and the Louisiana Territory, behind them and ventured onto foreign soil for the first time—though exactly whose soil it was no one could say with certainty.

The next day, Lewis had a shocking conversation with Charbonneau. He casually mentioned to Lewis that the Shoshones were planning to abandon the expedition the next day and start their buffalo hunt. How did he know this, Lewis asked. Sacagawea had heard the Shoshone discussing their plans early that morning and had reported to her husband. Lewis was furious that Charbonneau had such little

At Lemhi Pass, Lewis finally reached the western edge of the Louisiana Purchase and U.S. territory. At the summit, he expected to see an easy, gradual slope that lead to the Columbia River. Instead, he saw row upon row of forbidding mountains. Photo by author.

comprehension of the crisis they now faced. He had sat on this vital information for nearly a day. If the Shoshone left, the men would be without means to get their supplies over the mountains and all hope of buying more horses would be lost. In short, it would likely mean the failure of the expedition.

Charbonneau's foolishness stands in marked contrast to Sacajawea's loyalty. She must have been deeply torn when she heard that Cameahwait planned to abandon the expedition. These were her people and they needed food, yet the white men needed their help to reach the ocean. She could have easily said nothing and allowed her people to return to Three Forks without Lewis' foreknowledge. For some reason, she

William Henry Jackson took this picture of a Shoshone camp in 1870 while traveling with a survey team in the Wind River Mountains. Lewis, Clark, Sacajawea, Charbonneau, and York slept in a teepee similar to these. The men slept in the open. Used by permission, Utah State Historical Society, all rights reserved.

determined to side with the white men. Perhaps the common sense of purpose and her fair treatment by the captains made Sacajawea think of herself as a member of the Corps of Discovery first and a Shoshone second. Maybe she didn't want to be stranded in the mountains along with her husband and baby. In either case, she gave Captain Lewis a chance to salvage the expedition.

Lewis quickly called a council. He asked the chiefs if they were men of their word. They answered yes. Then why were they planning to abandon the expedition? Cameahwait's honor was now at stake. He apologized and promised Lewis

The most physically demanding portion of the expedition was the crossing of Lolo Pass. The forest was thick. The terrain was steep. Game was almost non-existent. Sacajawea made the crossing while caring for a baby. Photo by author.

that he would keep his agreement. A few days later, they reached the village and traded for every horse the Shoshone's could spare. Prices had gone up. The Shoshones knew that the expedition needed horses at any price and there were no other sellers. Clark parted with a pistol, a knife, and a hundred rounds of ammunition for just one horse. In the end, they were only able to acquire 29 horses and many of them were weak or injured.

An old Shoshone, who had once crossed the Rocky Mountains as a young man, agreed to lead the party. The captains nicknamed him, "Old Toby." Finally, the Shoshones were free to leave the white men and begin the annual buffalo hunt. Sacajawea said good-bye to her native people and headed the opposite direction with a group of white men she had met less than a year before.

Why didn't Sacajawea stay with her people? Sacajawea was thrilled to be re-united with the Shoshone, yet she left them and continued on with her husband and the Corps of Discovery. Perhaps she felt that she had no choice. She was obligated to Charbonneau. The more likely explanation is that, however much she loved her people, her life was better among the white men. She had enough to eat. She did not live in constant fear of enemies. Her child would have opportunities impossible for the Shoshones to even imagine. There is one other factor though it is purely speculation: she may have wanted to finish the journey. Sacajawea had struggled through hundreds of miles of adventures with the Corps of Discovery. Maybe she wanted to see the ocean and complete the adventure she had begun. Maybe the curiosity of the Corps of Discovery had rubbed off on her.

Chapter 6
To the Pacific

From Lolo Pass to Fort Clatsop
September 1805-March 1806

September 1805 was the most difficult month of the entire journey. Sacajawea's fellow Shoshone, Old Toby, guided the men through the Bitterroot Mountains and then across Lolo Pass in the panhandle of present-day Idaho. He wasn't an ideal guide. Many years had passed since he had covered the trail. More than once he led them on time-consuming and grueling detours. The terrain was so rugged that the horses would sometimes lose their footing and roll down the mountainside. Snow had already started falling and had driven most of the game to lower elevations. Several times they were forced to kill horses for food. The men were exhausted, cold, hungry, and often sick. Sacajawea endured the same hardships as the men, all the time carrying and nursing a baby.

Finally, the Corps of Discovery reached a Nez Perce village. Like the Shoshone, the Nez Perce encountered a group of weak and vulnerable strangers who desperately needed their help to survive. The wise choice would have

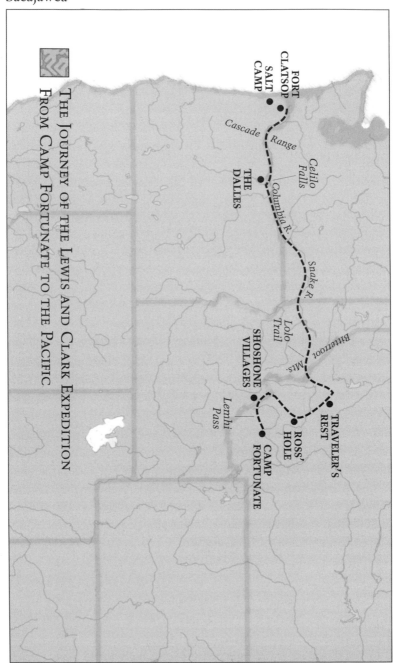

THE JOURNEY OF THE LEWIS AND CLARK EXPEDITION
FROM CAMP FORTUNATE TO THE PACIFIC

FORT
CLATSOP

SALT
CAMP

Cascade Range

Celilo
Falls

THE
DALLES

Columbia R.

Snake R.

Lolo
Trail

Bitterroot Mts.

SHOSHONE
VILLAGES

Lemhi
Pass

TRAVELER'S
REST

ROSS'
HOLE

CAMP
FORTUNATE

been to slaughter them and take their weapons and trade goods. Instead, the Nez Perce befriended the expedition. They fed them. They showed the white men how to burn out the interior of a log to make a canoe and they agreed to tend the expedition's horses until they returned the next year. A few of the Nez Perce chiefs even accompanied them for several hundred miles.

Near present-day Orofino, Idaho, the Corps of Discovery returned to water travel on the Clearwater River. Jefferson's hope for an easy portage between the Columbia and Missouri River systems had been thoroughly dashed by the real world geography of the Rocky Mountains; but at least Lewis and Clark had proven that the portage was possible. Now they were moving downstream. Instead of pushing, pulling, and poling their way up the Missouri, they were being hurtled down the steep grade of the Clearwater, Snake, and Columbia Rivers. Because of their rush to reach the Pacific before winter, they often shot through rapids that the local Indian tribes considered un-navigable.

They made excellent progress. Just one month after shoving their canoes into the Clearwater River, Clark exclaimed in his journal entry of November 7th, "Ocian in view! O! the joy." The joy didn't last long. For two days, the expedition was pinned against the stone walls of the Columbia River estuary, unable to go forward or backward. Even after they managed to escape, the expedition moved from one bad campsite to another. All the time they were wet and cold. The captains eventually decided to vote on where they would spend the winter. Even Sacajawea and York were allowed to vote, decades before the other members of their race and gender were allowed that privilege. The party voted to explore the southern side of the Columbia River and build a fort there if practical. They built Fort Clatsop (named for the local Indian tribe) near the present town of Astoria, Oregon and moved in on Christmas Eve.

The Corps of Discovery spent the winter of 1805-1806 at a log structure they built themselves named Fort Clatsop. The National Park Service has built a replica of that building near Astoria, Oregon. Courtesy of Fort Clatsop National Memorial, National Park Service.

On Christmas Day, Lewis and Clark gave all the men some tobacco or handkerchiefs. Even this small gift was a sacrifice. They had few trade goods to spare and the Indians were skilled traders. Sacajawea gave Clark a gift of two-dozen weasel tails, by far the most generous present among those listed by Clark.

Was Sacajawea romantically involved with Clark? Sacajawea's gift to Clark and his exceptional treatment towards her have prompted some biographers to assume that there was a romantic relationship between the two. There are slight indications. Clark gave Sacajawea a nickname. A few weeks before the Christmas present, she gave a Clark a piece of bread she had been carefully saving for Little Pomp. There is also an unusual Clark journal entry for November 14: "Squaw displeased with me." We have no idea why she was displeased, yet this brief entry is insightful. Sacajawea must have told Clark about her feelings. This seems unusual for a repressed Indian woman to criticize the leader of the expedition. It also seems unusual that Clark would care what she thought and care enough to mention the episode in the journals. He never bothered to make a notation when any other member of the Corps of Discovery was displeased with him.

There is no doubt that Clark had a special attachment to Sacajawea, but it also extended to the entire Charbonneau family. After the expedition, he made a considerable effort to help set up Charbonneau as a farmer and to raise Jean-Baptiste as an educated aristocrat like himself. His feelings towards Sacajawea were probably more paternal than romantic. He saw an intelligent and brave teenage girl who had had a difficult life. She had been of great service to him on the expedition. The baby, Little Pomp, had cheered his heart during the journey. Clark was just a nice guy who wanted to help some very close friends. He probably saw Sacajawea and thought of his own sweetheart, Julia Hancock--for whom the Judith River is named in Montana. Upon his return to the United States, Clark promptly married Julia and started a family.

The expedition had a little excitement in early January. The Clatsops reported that a whale had washed ashore just a few miles south of camp. Clark decided to head a party to harvest some of the blubber. When Sacajawea learned that she was not to be included, she made her feelings known. "She observed that She had traveled a long way with us to See the great waters, and that now that monstrous fish was also to be Seen, She thought it verry hard that She Could not be permitted to See either." Clark agreed. Sacajawea was allowed to come along. This episode is also insightful into the personality of Sacajawea. Many of the men did not even bother to make the short trip from Fort Clatsop to see the ocean, yet this Indian woman's curiosity would not allow her to miss the opportunity. At this point, Sacajawea joins the Corps of Discovery not just in body but also in spirit.

Chapter 7

Back to the Mandan Villages

From Fort Clatsop to the Mandan Villages
April-August 1806

After two years away from their families and friends, the men of the Corps of Discovery were ready to return home. The journal entries during the Fort Clatsop months sometimes sound like homesick kids reporting to their parents on a summer camp experience gone horribly awry. The food was bad. The weather was bad. Even the girls were bad. (Lewis had to forbid the men from fraternizing with the Indian women for fear of venereal disease.) They had camped near the coast in the hope that a British or American trading ship would pass nearby and carry them back to the states. That never happened. There was no choice but to return by the same route they had come.

They traveled up the Columbia River for a month, living mostly on dog meat. When some Indians stole Lewis' huge Newfoundland, Seaman—probably for their own dinner—Lewis snapped. Indians had been stealing small items for some time and this was one theft he could not tolerate. He sent three men after the thieves and gave them

49

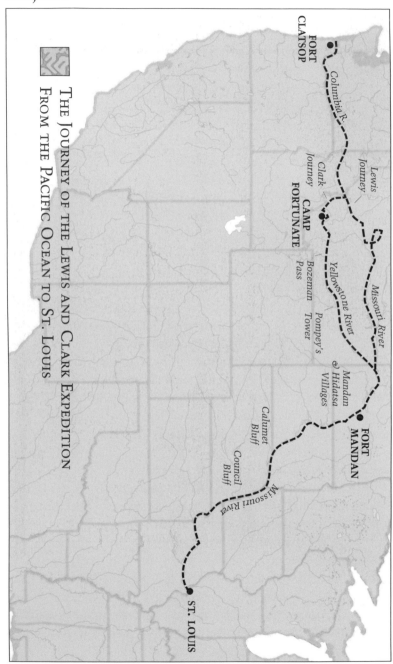

THE JOURNEY OF THE LEWIS AND CLARK EXPEDITION
FROM THE PACIFIC OCEAN TO ST. LOUIS

FORT CLATSOP

Columbia R.

Lewis Journey

Clark Journey

CAMP FORTUNATE

Bozeman Pass

Yellowstone River

Missouri River

Pompey's Tower

Mandan & Hidatsa Villages

FORT MANDAN

Calumet Bluff

Council Bluff

Missouri River

ST. LOUIS

Edward S. Curtis photographed PioPio-Maksmaks, a member of the
Walla Walla tribe. The Walla Wallas were among the many tribes who
helped the Corps of Discovery complete their journey.
Photo from the Library of Congress, Prints and Photographs Division,
LC-USZ-62-52475.

permission to shoot if the Indians put up the slightest resistance. The Indians wisely released the dog and ran away. Lewis was not the only man frustrated with the Indians. At the end of the day he wrote, "our men seem well disposed to kill a few of them."

At the end of April, their luck with Indians changed. They met up with Chief Yellept and the Walla Wallas. The chief presented Clark with a "very elegant" white horse. Clark gave the chief his sword. Chief Yellept instructed his people to be friendly to the white men. The Walla Wallas shared their food and even some horses. There was a Shoshone woman among the Walla Wallas, so Sacajawea was once again able to serve as interpreter, albeit through a five-language chain. Based on advice from the Indians, Lewis and Clark decided to use their horses to take a quicker, overland route to the mountains.

The expedition soon reached the Nez Perce and the rest of their horses. Sacajawea became chief interpreter again when they discovered that this tribe also had a Shoshone. Here, the iron baby of the frontier finally became sick. Little Pomp was stricken with a high fever and a swollen neck and throat. For five days, Lewis treated him with a hot poultice of boiled onions, cream of tartar, and enemas. Whether the treatments made his condition better or worse is debatable, but Jean-Baptiste finally did recover.

On the return trip across Lolo Pass, the captains wisely employed Nez Perce guides. The trip took only six days this time and required little of the hardship that attended the previous year's passage with Old Toby. Once over the mountains, Lewis and Clark decided to split the party. Lewis would go overland to the Great Falls, then explore the Marias River north to see if the Louisiana Purchase entitled the United States to any Canadian territory. Clark would mostly follow their previous route to the south and then explore the Yellowstone River. They planned to meet in about a month at

The Northern Pacific Railroad follows the Bozeman Pass through
Montana re-tracing the same route Sacajawea showed to William Clark.
Photo from the Library of Congress, Prints and Photographs Division,
LC-USF34-027252-D.

the mouth of the Yellowstone. As usual, Sacajawea went with
Clark.

For the next few weeks Sacajawea was able to help direct
the party. This was probably the only time that she acted as a
guide. Clark noted her contribution in the journals: "The
Indian woman who has been of great Service to me as a pilot
through this Country recommends a gap in the mountains
more South which I shall cross." Sacajawea was pointing
towards Bozeman Pass, a course that saved the expedition
valuable time.

On July 25th, the Yellowstone River took them by a
remarkable rock formation. A large circular pillar rose 200
feet, straight out of the flat riverbed. The landmark could be

ascended on one side and provided an excellent view of the surrounding plain. Clark named the spot, Pompy's Tower" for little Jean-Baptiste. Since then the name has changed to "Pompey's Pillar." Like any good explorer, Clark carved his initials in the sandstone side of the column. The inscription can still be seen today.

By early August, Clark's group had reached the rendezvous point, but there was no sign of Lewis. It was almost two weeks before they spotted his boats floating down the Missouri. Lewis was lying face down in one of the canoes. He was shot. The assailant was one of his own men, Pierre Cruzatte. They had been hunting together and Cruzatte, who was blind in one eye and near-sighted in the other, mistook Lewis for an elk. Lewis spent the next couple weeks painfully healing from this bullet wound through the buttocks.

The reunited Corps of Discovery wasted little time swapping stories. They continued down the Missouri at record pace, making 86 miles the next day. The following day they paddled into the Mandan villages and fired their guns in salute. Sacajawea was home. After four days of councils and trading the expedition continued on to St. Louis. This was a sad parting, more for Sacajawea than the men. The Americans were returning home as heroes and would be receiving land grants and cash. Sacajawea was returning to the mundane life of a trapper's wife. Lewis paid Charbonneau $500 for his services. Sacajawea received nothing.

Clark would have liked Charbonneau to return to the states as a paid interpreter for one of the Minnetaree chiefs, who would then travel on to Washington to meet the President. Unfortunately, none of the Minnetaree chiefs could be persuaded to make the journey, and Clark could not legitimately pay Charbonneau when he had no use for him. Had this worked out, Sacajawea might have met Thomas Jefferson. Clark invited the Charbonneaus to come to St. Louis as private citizens but they declined. Charbonneau was a mountain man. He had no desire to live in the city. Clark offered to take Pomp and raise him as his own son. The Charbonneaus agreed to bring him to Clark in a year. With that understanding, they parted.

Could the expedition have succeeded without Sacajawea? We can never know the answer to hypothetical questions like this with certainty but if I was a gambler, I'd bet against Lewis and Clark. Let's concede that the expedition would have somehow survived without Sacajawea's food-gathering, nursing, sewing, and cooking--though they certainly would have been less comfortable. But there are two occasions, and possibly a third, in which Sacajawea's role was nearly indispensable. At Camp Fortunate, Cameahwait would have surely been helpful, but would he have willingly depleted his horse herd and postponed the buffalo hunt unless his own sister had asked him? Lewis would have had much difficulty pleading his case through Drouillard's awkward hand signals rather than Sacajawea's native Shoshone. Later, when Cameahwait planned to slip away and strand Lewis on Lemhi pass, Sacajawea's advance warning allowed him the opportunity to salvage the situation. Finally, on the Weippe prairie, when the Nez Perce could have easily massacred the expedition, Indian legend suggests that Sacajawea's presence calmed the warriors. The Indians had never seen a war party with a woman and a baby. A Nez Perce woman was able to convince the tribe that Lewis and Clark had peaceful intentions. There is no doubt that Clark considered Sacajawea a valuable, perhaps indispensable, member of the Corps of Discovery. When she was near death at Sulfur Springs, Lewis' anxious journal entries indicate that he felt the same.

Three days later, Clark was still feeling bad about leaving the Charbonneaus behind. He missed them, and worried that he would never see his dear friends again. In their two years together, Clark had come to think of them as family. He composed a letter to Charbonneau, which he sent upriver with a trader. In the letter he tried every conceivable means to convince Charbonneau to come to St. Louis. He promised to set him up as a farmer, loan him a horse to visit Montreal, and partner with him in a trading business with the Minnetarees. Clark also apologized for not paying Sacajawea. "Your woman, who accompanied you that long and fatiguing route to the Pacific Ocian and back, deserved a greater reward for her attention and service on that route than we had power to give her at the Mandans." This was an inequity Clark hoped to right at some future time. He poignantly ended the letter, "Wishing you and your family great success, and with anxious expectations of seeing my little dancing boy, Baptiste, I shall remain your friend." Clark would soon get his wish.

Chapter 8
Life After the Expedition

There are few undisputed facts about Sacajawea's life after the separation at the Mandan villages. Most historians agree that Charbonneau took Sacajawea and Jean-Baptiste to St. Louis towards the end of 1806 to visit Clark and start a new life. He didn't stay long. Soon, he was off to the Southwest on a fur-trapping expedition. Presumably, Sacajawea stayed behind in St. Louis though we know nothing of what her life was like there. It's hard to imagine that it wasn't lonely without her husband, living in such a totally foreign environment. In 1810, Charbonneau bought some land from Clark, apparently with the intention of becoming a farmer. That lasted about six months. He sold the land back to Clark in the spring of 1811.

Leaving Jean-Baptiste in St. Louis to be raised by Clark, he headed back up the Missouri with Sacajawea. Also on the boat was a lawyer from Pittsburgh named Henry Brackenridge who later published his journals. Brackenridge's brief paragraph is the longest description of Sacajawea since the expedition:

"We have on board a Frenchman named Charbonet, with his wife, an Indian woman of the Snake nation, both of whom accompanied Lewis and Clark to the Pacific, and were of great service. The woman, a good creature of mild and gentle disposition, was greatly attached to the whites, whose manners and aims she tried to imitate; but she had become sickly and longed to revisit her native country; her husband also, who had spent many years amongst the Indians, was become weary of a civilized life."

Brackenridge's analysis has the ring of truth. Sacajawea probably made a valiant attempt to fit into white society in St. Louis but ultimately felt more comfortable among the Indians. Sacajawea was, in a sense, the ultimate displaced person. She was a Shoshone captive among the Minnetarees, an emissary for the white men when she returned to her own people, and an isolated Indian in white St. Louis. Even in her own marriage, she was separated by age and culture. Given these misfortunes, a reasonable person might assume she felt unhappy and exploited. Yet that doesn't seem to be the case. At least, that doesn't seem to be how she thought of herself. Based on her assertive actions among the Corps of Discovery and Brackenridge's comments about her "white dress and mannerisms," she was a person who was strong enough to adapt to the various demanding situations in which she found herself. She was not self-pitying. Throughout the expedition, the captains commented on her cheerfulness. She was also generous to others. Clark was a good judge of character, and he thought highly of her.

The Charbonneaus made their way up the Missouri and settled at Fort Lisa near the border of North and South Dakota. Again, Charbonneau left to trap. While he was away, the illness that Brackenridge had mentioned must have worsened. Sacajawea died on December 12, 1812. William Luttig, the clerk at Fort Lisa, recorded that: "This evening the wife of Charbonneau, a Snake squaw, died of a putrid fever. She was a good and the best woman in the fort, aged about 25 years. She left a fine infant girl." Luttig took the

Many Shoshone believe that Sacajawea is buried here at the Shoshone Indian Cemetary on the Wind River Indian Reservation. Photo from the Library of Congress, Prints and Photographs Division, HABS, WYO, 7-FOWA,V,1-1.

baby, Lizette, back to St. Louis where she and Jean-Baptiste were eventually adopted by Clark.

There are competing theories about Sacajawea's death. According to an oral tradition among the Indians, Sacajawea lived to be nearly a hundred years old, and is buried on the Wind River Indian Reservation. A gravestone on the reservation supports this theory. The woman that sailed with Brackenridge and died at Fort Lisa is assumed to be Charbonneau's other Shoshone wife, Otter Woman. We will never know for sure, but the consensus of most scholars is that it was Sacajawea who died at Fort Lisa. Clark also believed that. Around 1825, he compiled a list of all the members of the Corps of Discovery, and listed their whereabouts. Sacajawea, along with many others, was listed as dead. Given

Clark's close association with the Charbonneaus and their children, it is extremely unlikely that he could be mistaken about her death.

Toussaint Charbonneau lived to be an old man, even as he continued to marry young Indian girls. A merchant at Fort Clark recorded in 1838—when Charbonneau was 75 years old—that "Charbonneau and his lady started for Gros Ventres on a visit (or to tell you the truth) in quest of one of his runway wives—for I must inform you he had two lively ones. Poor old man." At age 79, he married an Assiniboine girl of fourteen. The date of his death and burial site are unknown.

Jean-Baptiste Charbonneau, or Little Pomp, lived a full, exciting life. He stayed in St. Louis as a youth and was educated at Clark's expense. At age 18, he and his father met the German Prince Paul of Wurttemberg. They served the prince as interpreters and guides. The prince took a liking to Jean-Baptiste and they became traveling companions on the American frontier and, later, in Europe. When he returned to America after five years, Jean-Baptiste was fluent in German, French, English, and Spanish. Born in an earth lodge in North Dakota to a teenage Indian mother, Jean-Baptiste Charbonneau now had all the advantages that education and influence could offer. He chose to become a mountain man like his father . . . well, not quite like his father. He was undoubtedly the most cultured mountain man any Indian or pioneer was likely to meet. Jean-Baptiste earned a reputation as one of the most skilled guides in the west. He knew Jim Bridger and Kit Carson. During the Mexican War, the Army hired him to lead the Mormon Battalion from Fort Leavenworth, Kansas to California. He stayed in California as the mayor of the San Luis Rey Mission. In his early sixties, he set off for the gold fields of Montana. Along the way, he died of pneumonia in southeastern Oregon. A historical marker designates the site.

Why is Sacajawea so revered today? Any impartial observer would have to admit that Sacajawea's lofty place in the national pantheon of heroes is obviously disproportionate to her contribution. There are more statues of her than any other woman in American history. Her selection for the dollar coin places her beside the likes of Washington, Jefferson, and Lincoln. She was a brave, resourceful, intelligent woman. She may have even facilitated the expansion of the American West by a few years, but none of her achievements can justify her enormous popularity.

The historical Sacajawea has long since been appropriated as a symbol. Because we know nothing about Sacajawea in her own voice, she has become infinitely malleable. At the turn of the century, she was a heroine for the women's suffrage movement. At times, she has been the willing Indian princess who helped the first white explorers conquer her native land. To others, she represents the white man's dependence on Native Americans.

All these roles are a heavy burden for any teenager to bear. In truth, Sacajawea was caught up in forces and events larger than herself. She survived, endured, and embraced physical and emotional hardships that would have destroyed most people. For this alone, she is worthy of our admiration.

Bibliography

Ambrose, Stephen E.
Undaunted Courage: Meriwether Lewis, Thomas Jefferson, and the Opening of the American West.
New York: Simon & Schuster, 1996.

Ambrose, Stephen E.
Lewis & Clark: Voyage of Discovery.
National Geographic Society, 1998.

Bakeless, John.
Lewis and Clark: Partners in Discovery.
New York: William Morrow & Company, 1947.

Clark, Ella E and Edmonds, Margot.
Sacagawea of the Lewis and Clark Expedition
University of California Press: Berkeley, 1979.

DeVoto, Bernard, Editor.
The Journals of Lewis and Clark
Boston: Houghton Mifflin Company, 1953.

Duncan, Dayton and Burns, Ken,
Lewis & Clark: The Journey of the Corps of Discovery
New York: Alfred A Knopf, 1997.

Howard, Harold P.
Sacajawea
University of Oklahoma Press: Norman, 1971.

Hunsaker, Joyce Badgley.
Sacagawea Speaks
Globe Pequot Press: Guilford, CT, 2001.

Jackson, Donald.
Letters of the Lewis and Clark Expedition
University of Illinois Press: Urbana, 1978.

Kessler, Donna J.
The Making of Sacagawea: A Euro-American Legend
University of Alabama Press: Tuscaloosa, 1996.

MacGregor, Carol Lynn, Editor.
The Journals of Patrick Gass
Missoula: Mountain Press Publishing, 1997.

Madsen, Brigham D.
The Lemhi: Sacajawea's People
Caxton Press: Caldwell, ID, 2000

Moulton, Gary, Editor.
The Journals of the Lewis & Clark Expedition
11 Volumes
Lincoln: University of Nebraska Press, 1986-1997

Slaughter, Thomas P.
Exploring Lewis and Clark
Alfred A. Knopf: New York, 2003.

Brad Phillips

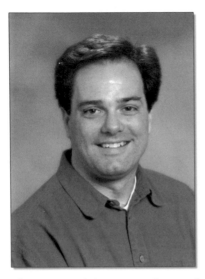 is currently working on a four-volume history of the Lewis and Clark Expedition, biographies of Sacajawea and York, and a book on the Indian tribes encountered by the expedition. At college, Brad studied Japanese and history, before graduating and moving to Eastern Washington to operate his own retail clothing stores.

Growing up and raising his family in the Pacific Northwest, Brad has had the chance to visit many places along the Lewis and Clark trail. He has camped along the Columbia River, rafted down the Salmon and Snake, and followed the trail over the Rocky Mountains.

Brad has written a weekly humor column about marriage and family issues for five years, and has also been a contributor to magazines and Internet sites. Currently, he lives in Salt Lake City, Utah with his wife and five children and is contemplating more adventures along the Lewis and Clark Trail.

Additional Apricot Press Books

'The American Pantry' Cookbooks

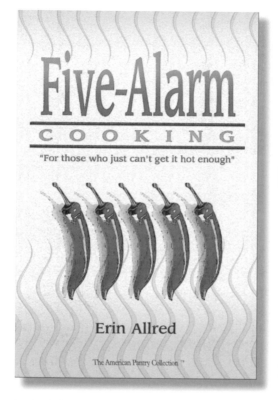

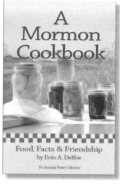

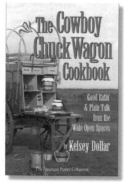

Order Online! www.apricotpress.com

'The Wayside Bookshop'

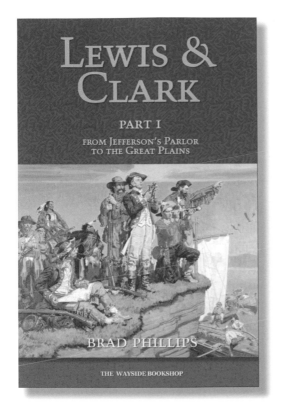

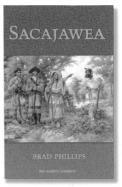

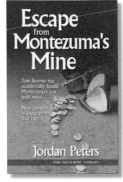

Additional Apricot Press Books

'The Truth About Life' Humor Books

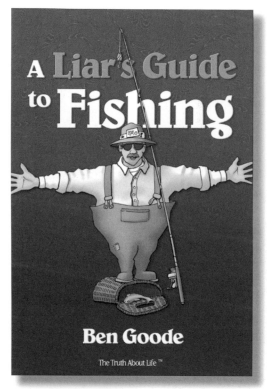

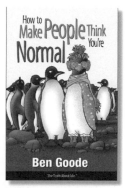

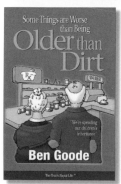

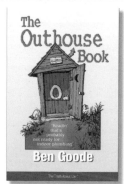

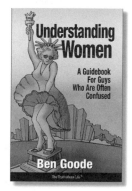

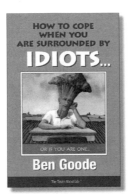

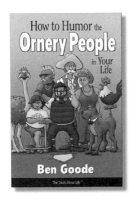

Additional Apricot Press Books

'The Wayside Bookshop'

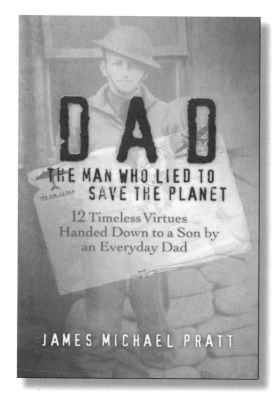

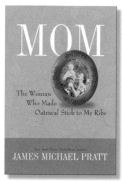

Apricot Press Order Form

Book Title	Quantity	x	Cost / Book	=	Total
_____	_____		_____		_____
_____	_____		_____		_____
_____	_____		_____		_____
_____	_____		_____		_____
_____	_____		_____		_____
_____	_____		_____		_____
_____	_____		_____		_____
_____	_____		_____		_____

All Cook Books are $9.95 US.   All other books are $6.95 US.

Do not send Cash. Mail check or money order to:
Apricot Press   P.O. Box 1611
American Fork, Utah   84003
Telephone 801-756-0456
Allow 3 weeks for delivery.

Quantity discounts available.
Call us for more information.
9 a.m. - 5 p.m. MST

Sub Total =

Shipping = $2.00

Tax 8.5% =

Total Amount Enclosed =

Shipping Address

Name:

Street:

City: State:

Zip Code:

Telephone:

Email: